Consider It Pure Joy

Not What I W...

Mary Slankster, Ed.D.

Inspiring Voices®

Inspiring Voices books may be ordered through
booksellers or by contacting:

Inspiring Voices
1663 Liberty Drive
Bloomington, IN 47403
www.inspiringvoices.com
844-686-9605

ISBN: 978-1-4624-1337-9 (sc)
ISBN: 978-1-4624-1336-2 (e)

Library of Congress Control Number: 2021912738

Print information available on the last page.

Inspiring Voices rev. date: 08/18/2021

Contents

Preface

In a small town on a cold Friday evening in late December, my groom and I sang to each other. My thoughts at that blissful moment were that this marriage would be a lifetime of serving God together, until *death do us part*. However, on a warm September Sunday afternoon, almost twenty-five years later, that song took on a new meaning. You see, I was served with divorce papers.

My husband, who had been an ordained minister for many years, had left me two and a half years earlier. Why would this happen to me when I was diligently trying to serve God? I may never fully understand, but I do know that James 1:2 tells us to "consider it pure joy … when you face trials of many kinds."[1]

I would not have chosen the path of divorce, but I would not take anything for what the Lord has taught me.

On the practical side, I learned how to take care of my car, the yard, and a backyard swimming pool as well as repair rental property when the renters trashed it out and didn't tell me they were leaving. After a hailstorm, I even learned how to select the best bid for roof repairs.

On the spiritual side, I learned, in greater depth, how to truly recognize, listen to, and obey God's voice. God spoke to me through His Word, songs, and many dreams. When God would wake me during the night, I learned to write down what He was saying to me.

In the first dream that God gave me during

---

[1] All scripture references will be from the Holy Bible, New International Version, unless otherwise noted.

this phase of my life, He told me to *safeguard the resources.* That dream, along with His Word and constantly seeking His wisdom, carried me through the three-year period of separation, which finally ended in divorce.

Prior to the divorce trial, God impressed on me *how* to safeguard the resources. Paul tells us in Hebrews 11:1, "Faith is confidence in what we hope for and assurance about what we do not see." When God speaks, refuse to doubt what He has said. By faith, I knew that the judge's ruling would concur with what God had *dropped into my heart.* Up to this time in my life, my faith had never been tested to this extent.

Acknowledgments

Thanks to my brothers and sisters, who encouraged me through this journey; my daughter, who walked with me through the journey; my former pastor, who recommended that I write down what God was teaching me; my colleagues at work and friends at church, for their encouragement and moral support during this difficult time in my life; my heavenly Father for being my husband; Jesus Christ, who never left me or forsook me; and the Holy Spirit, for being my comforter during the grieving process.

Introduction

Divorce is one of the most painful experiences I have ever had. The divorce decree brought death to the marriage but no closure to the heart. The former way of life was over. The hurt went deep, with doubts that the heart would ever heal.

When divorce shattered my dreams and tore our family apart, I had a choice. I could become either bitter or better. I chose the latter, and that has made all the difference.

Since that eventful day, many hurting people have come my way. Aching and alone, they are grieving over some type of loss: divorce, death of a loved one, loss of a job, abandonment, abuse, loss of health, loss of finances. The list seems endless.

Through some of the things I experienced and learned, God has given me a greater empathy to minister to others. As I walked through many different stages during the three-year separation and then the divorce, I experienced a variety of feelings, all the way from denial to acceptance. I had to give myself time to heal. I had to accept a new identity in society.

Instead of being swallowed in a sea of self-pity, I chose to mourn positively, which allowed me to feel the loss and sorrow yet still remember the good times of our marriage. Sure, I hurt and experienced an empty space in my life, but divorce, or any other type of loss, cannot kill that inner joy that comes from God.

Regardless of your loss, *Consider It Pure Joy* brings you hope. Some of you may have already experienced a similar loss. Others may be experiencing it now. Still others may experience it in the future. Or perhaps you know someone who is going through or will go through similar circumstances. May God use these thoughts to help you in your loss and perhaps help you to assist others in their journey.

1

Denial

I will praise the Lord, who counsels
me; even at night my heart instructs
me. I keep my eyes always on the
Lord. With him at my right hand, I
will not be shaken.
—Psalm 16:7–8 (NIV)

When my husband left me after twenty-two years of
marriage, I denied that it could be happening. We
had worked side by side in ministry all our married
life. This just could not be happening! Our marriage
could not become one of those sad statistics!

Denying the situation, though, did not make it
go away. I had to face the facts. The facts were that

the separation lasted for a long three years before the divorce decree was issued. In the state where we lived, there was no such marital status as legal separation. Until we were divorced, we were still legally married, which really complicated matters during the period of separation.

Inward emotions ran the gamut. Shock! Daze! Anger! Loneliness! Rejection! These feelings, along with many others, differed considerably from the feelings of optimism and hope with which our marriage began.

The first step in dealing with the circumstances was admitting that the situation really existed. That was the only way I could grow. This *was* happening to me. Denying it would not make it go away. I was in divorce country regardless of whether or not I wanted to be. Reading Jim Smoke's book, *Growing through Divorce*, was very helpful. Smoke said, "[Divorce is] a strange place with different rules, regulations, and road signs. You want it all to change and go away. But it won't!"[2]

As I read and applied the concepts in the Working Guide of Smoke's book, I learned more about myself and learned to be patient with myself. Growth is a process. It doesn't all just happen overnight. It takes time to grow. Leaning on the Holy Spirit's wisdom, I learned to set goals for myself and that, through the Holy Spirit's help, I could achieve these goals.

Smoke said that "shock is accepting the facts of divorce and adjusting is doing something about it."[3] He introduced the possibilities of positive or negative mourning. In choosing to mourn positively, I said the following statements aloud as an act of self-emancipation: "I'm sorry that the good times are gone now, but I know that there is still much

---

[2] Jim Smoke, *Growing through Divorce* (Eugene, OR: Harvest House Publishers, 1995), 9.

[3] Smoke, *Growing through Divorce,* 173.

happiness left for me in life. I hurt, and for now there is an empty space in my life."[4]

I chose not to mourn negatively and have multiple pity parties. Instead, when I did feel sorry for myself, I chose to limit myself to fifteen seconds of self-pity. Smoke gave me pairs of sentences from which to choose. I chose the latter of each pair.

- Hating yourself. Or Learning to like yourself.
- Refusing to believe you'll survive. Or Believing not that you'll merely survive, but that you'll emerge healthier and stronger than before.
- Thinking of divorce as negative and self-defeating. Or Looking at divorce as an experience which can help you grow.[5]

Another book that was extremely encouraging to me was Dr. George O. Wood's *A Psalm in Your Heart, Volume 1, Psalms 1–75*. Wood said, "We will have many different reactions to loss. David's psalm reflects a continuum—denial, despair,

---

[4] Smoke, *Growing through Divorce*, 174.

[5] Smoke, *Growing through Divorce*, 176.

anger, hurt, sorrow, grief, and acceptance. Psalm 16 shows us what we will feel like when we finally reach inner resolution on our life crises."[6]

As I worked through the denial stage, my life seemed like a giant jigsaw puzzle. The most difficult pieces of the puzzle ranged from disorganization, distractions, and loneliness to just being a single mom. At least I did not have to change jobs, which was a blessing. Also, changing houses and moving was postponed until after the divorce was final.

The words of "The Broken Vessel,"[7] a song that I had sung many times, were comforting to me. God did truly "pick up the pieces of my broken heart." I just had to remember once again Jeremiah's illustration of the potter and the clay in Jeremiah, chapter 18. The clay does not tell the potter what vessel he wants to be. The potter

[6] George O. Wood, *A Psalm in Your Heart, Volume 1, Psalms 1–75* (Springfield, MO: Gospel Publishing House, 1997), 65.

[7] Andraé Crouch, "The Broken Vessel" (Pacific City, OR: Manna Music, Inc. 1968).

makes that decision. My heavenly Father knew when I was in my mother's womb His purpose for creating me. My role was just in surrendering my will to His and allowing Him to mold and make me into the vessel of His choosing.

Prayer

Thank You, Lord, for helping me to face the facts throughout this period of denial. I praise You for Your counsel and wisdom during the difficult days. Please help me to be all that You created me to be. In Jesus's name. Amen!

Reflection Questions

1. During a time of loss, do you remember going through a denial phase?
   a. If so, how did you respond?
   b. If so, how should you have responded?
2. What did you learn during the denial phase that could be of benefit to someone else?

2

Reconciliation

Be kind and compassionate to one
another, forgiving each other, just
as in Christ God forgave you.
—Ephesians 4:32 (NIV)

I would like to be writing this chapter telling you
that after a three-year separation, our marriage
was successful at reconciliation. In fact, I thought
that would be the case and we would be in ministry
together today, helping other couples reconcile
their marriages.

On Father's Day, two years before my husband

left the marriage, I gave him a card that read as follows:

> I can't tell you how blessed I feel to have you for my husband … You've always loved me, you've always been there when I needed you, and you've always made our times together as a family so special. Father's Day is a good day to tell you how grateful and happy I am that we're together. You're a wonderful husband and father, and I love you so very much.[8]

Only a year before leaving me, he had given me a birthday card with the following words: "I cannot promise you a life of sunshine … riches, wealth, or gold … an easy pathway that leads away from change or growing old. But I can promise all my heart's devotion, a smile to chase away your tears of sorrow, a love that's ever true and ever growing, A hand to hold in yours through each tomorrow …"[9] He signed the card *Your loving husband.*

---

[8] *American Greetings* card.

[9] *Classic Elegance American Greetings,* Cleveland, Ohio.

Eleven months after he left, he agreed to reconcile and indicated that he wanted to make our marriage work. Our daughter was so delighted. She told most of her friends at school that her mom and dad were getting back together, and she also requested prayer in her youth group at church. Three days later, he changed his mind. She came to me afterward crying and said that she needed a hug. We hugged each other, cried, and prayed together.

For another six months, I had high hopes of reconciliation. However, it takes both husband and wife to be willing to reconcile and restore the marriage. The youth pastor, having come from a broken home himself, said that it takes two people to get married, but it takes only one person to file for a divorce.

Some people believe if you pray hard enough and *really* believe, God will restore the marriage. Jim Smoke said that, after working in the divorce-recovery field for the past twenty years, "The other person you might still want to be married to has made a bad choice in leaving you, but you now have to live out his or her bad choice."[10] God did not make humans as robots. He gives each person the ability to choose. As a Christian, you should pray and believe. However, you "are often forced to live out someone else's decision."[11]

When my husband petitioned for a divorce, I knew at that point reconciliation was not a possibility. I received the petition on a Sunday afternoon in September. When the courier rang the doorbell to serve the petition, I was at the piano, practicing songs for the evening service. At that time, I was the music pastor at our church. The song that the doorbell interrupted was "I Came to Glorify His Name": "I came to glorify His Name … whoso offereth praise glorifieth Him … and to Him

---

[10] Smoke, *Growing through Divorce,* 153.

[11] Smoke, *Growing through Divorce*, 153.

who orders his conversation right, will I show the salvation of the Lord."[12] That song reflects the desire of my heart, and I hope it does yours too.

Perhaps you are reading this chapter and wondering if marriage separation can lead to reconciliation. The answer is *yes*, if very clear guidelines are set and followed by both partners.

Marriages fail for many reasons. Sometimes, "a temporary separation provides relief, a space for repentance, spiritual renewal, and an opportunity for recommitment." The marriage may be "so emotionally charged that the couple may benefit from a time-out to allow emotions to subside and rationality to reemerge." The risk of separation, though, "is that many couples simply use separation

---

[12] "I Came to Glorify His Name," accessed January 4, 2019, http://stevencarr.com/songs/worshipsongs.

as a prelude to getting comfortable living apart before they actually divorce."[13]

If a couple uses a separation period to work toward reconciliation, the counselor should do the following for the couple:[14]

- Draw up a separation contract that includes prayer, mutual agreements, care for the children, and agreement on sexual relations during separation (only with each other, of course). Explain the risks of separation.
- Remind the couple that separation is not divorce. There is to be no dating (others) or financial irresponsibility (e.g. a spouse may use the separation as an excuse to clean out bank accounts).
- Provide a clear timeline for the separation.
- Help the couple reflect on why they got married in the first place.
- Encourage the couple to seek the Holy Spirit to do deep personal spiritual evaluation that may include fasting. During this time they should keep a daily journal. One important question to reflect on during separation is, "What would I most need to change in myself

---

[13] "Healing Love's Wounds," accessed November 12, 2020, https://emerge.org/healing-loves-wounds-a-pastoral-approach-to-marriage-divorce-and-remarriage-counseling/.

[14] "Healing Love's Wounds."

to be successfully married to anyone? What is it in my spouse that most pleases the heart of God?" (This last bulleted item is a recommendation from John Gottman.[15])

Making the decision to move from separation to reconciliation does not happen overnight, but couples who work together can build stronger marriages.

Prayer

Heavenly Father, thank You for helping my faith in You not to waver as I was forced to live with the decision that my husband made when he chose to leave the marriage. Your grace was truly sufficient. Help my life to always glorify You. In Jesus's name. Amen!

---

[15] John Gottman, *The Marriage Clinic: A Scientifically Based Marital Therapy* (New York: Norton, 1999), quoted in "Healing Love's Wounds," accessed November 12, 2020, https://emerge.org/healing-loves-wounds-a-pastoral-approach-to-marriage-divorce-and-remarriage-counseling/.

Reflection Questions

1. What are some reasons for a temporary marriage separation?

2. What are some risks of a marriage separation?

3. How can a marriage separation lead to reconciliation?

3

Grief

So do not fear, for I am with you; do
not be dismayed, for I am your God.
I will strengthen you and help you;
I will uphold you with my righteous
right hand.
—Isaiah 41:10 (NIV)

I stayed in the grieving stage too long, and it almost killed me. The hurting in my chest became so severe that I thought I was going to have a heart attack. I went to the doctor for an EKG and MRI. It was just GERD (reflux), which was a result of excessive crying and trying to eat at the same time!

Through medication and much prayer from

my friends, God brought me through. My pastor preached a wonderful sermon on the second Sunday in February about Jesus's struggle in the Garden of Gethsemane and about His prayer of surrender, commitment, and resolution to do the Father's will. I felt an urgency to go forward during the altar call to renew my commitment to God to accomplish what He wanted me to do.

A great source of strength during this grieving stage was Dr. George O. Wood's book, *A Psalm in Your Heart, Volume 1, Psalms 1–75.* Wood commented:

> Our society is filled with spouses who have betrayed or hurt each other, parents who have abandoned children, children who have turned against parents, friends who have fallen out with one another. When you are on the receiving end of such hurtful conduct, your sole consolation may be that, when the one you love

has drawn away from you, the Lord
has drawn even closer to you.[16]

Often, during this difficult time of my life, I felt
as if I was facing more than I could handle. That's
when one of Wood's comments from Psalm 13
comforted me:

> Grief only occurs when there is
> the loss of something or someone
> precious. This loss may be a person,
> an expectation, a thing. The more
> value we attach to what is lost, the
> greater our depression. We need,
> like Martha, to believe Jesus is
> "the resurrection and the life" (John
> 11:25).[17]

So, how can you cope with loss? Wood said that
"Psalm 16 is written for people who have nothing
left but God."[18] Jesus even received comfort from

---

[16] Wood, *A Psalm in Your Heart,* 18.

[17] Wood, *A Psalm in Your Heart*, 54.

[18] Wood, *A Psalm in Your Heart*, 65.

Psalm 16:10, "You will not abandon me to the grave."

Ken Moses, a psychologist who has devoted his life to helping people deal with grief, said, "Grieving is an unlearned, spontaneous, and self-sufficient process … that facilitate[s] separation from a lost dream." Moses also indicated that the process not only facilitates letting go of the lost dream but also acquiring new, more attainable dreams.[19]

Two years after my divorce, one of my best friends was going through a difficult time. She had lost her husband through death. Also, one of her grandsons was born four months premature. Having just retired from teaching, she spent much of her time caring for the infant and taking him to the doctor. In an email to me, she said, "You seem so all together and brave through all that you have

---

[19] Ken Moses, "The Impact of Childhood Disability: The Parent's Struggle," accessed November 19, 2020, http://www.pent.ca.gov/beh/dis/parentstruggle_DK.pdf.

been through. There are times that I just fall apart. Guess a little prayer for me today would be good."[20]

I responded to my friend, "If I seem to be brave and have it all together, it is only my trust in the Lord. Time also has a way of healing."[21] I encouraged her to keep a log of what God was teaching her during this time. Doing so would be a great help to her and would also help her to minister to others in the future.

I prayed for my friend after reading her email and shared, "I know God is with you during this painful journey that you are traveling. Remember, though, that God will 'never leave you nor forsake you'" (Heb. 13:5). He is always there, and he knows the pain that you are feeling.[22] I shared with her the poem "Take Things One Day at a Time." A meaningful excerpt is: "As you begin your journey

---

[20] Friend's email to author.

[21] Author's email to friend

[22] Author's email to friend.

to recovery. Know that there are people with you every step of the way. Take just one day at a time … Believe in yourself. Believe you will win this battle and emerge better and stronger than ever."[23]

During this same season in her life, I also shared with her another poem, "My Authentic Self." This poem began with "In time, you will smile again and truly feel it, and your laughter will be genuine" and concluded with "You'll find a new strength, a new peace, and a new happiness. It just takes a little time."[24]

When someone you know experiences grief, how can you show, in positive ways, that you care? Dr. Alan D. Wolfelt,[25] a practicing grief counselor who also serves as director of the Center for Loss

---

[23] Ronnie M. Janney, "Take Things One Day at a Time," *One Step at a Time* (Boulder, CO: Blue Mountain Press, 1994), 8.

[24] Laurie Wymer, "My Authentic Self," *One Step at a Time* (Boulder, CO: Blue Mountain Press, 1994), 9.

[25] Alan D. Wolfelt, "Helping a Friend in Grief," accessed November 19, 2020, https://www.monarchsociety.com/griefarticle/article/helping10.

and Life Transition in Fort Collins, Colorado, gave some great advice. Here are some of his key points: (1) listen with your heart; (2) be compassionate; (3) avoid clichés; (4) understand the uniqueness of grief; (5) offer practical help; (6) make contact; (7) write a personal note; (8) be aware of holidays and anniversaries; and (9) understand the importance of the loss.

Helping a grieving friend is not easy. However, it is rewarding. Give of yourself, and allow God to help you be not only sympathetic but also empathetic.

The apostle Paul, who struggled with hardship and loss throughout his life, said in Romans 8:38–39, "For I am convinced that neither death nor life, neither angels nor demons, neither the present nor the future, nor any powers, neither height nor depth, nor anything else in all creation, will be able to separate us from the love of God that is in Christ Jesus our Lord."

Haddon W. Robinson, a distinguished professor at Gordon-Conwell Seminary, said, "Christians with this unflinching faith in the sovereign God do not deny grief. But even in their darkest, most wrenching hours, they borrow God's Strength. In their tears and pain they cling to God who will never let them go."[26]

Prayer

Thank You, God, that I do not have to fear during a time of loss. Thank You for Your strength during the grieving process. I praise You for healing me physically and emotionally and drawing me closer to you. You are an awesome God. In Jesus's name. Amen!

Reflection Questions

1. Have you ever experienced grief?

---

[26] Haddon W. Robinson, *Grief* (Grand Rapids, MI: Discovery House Publishers, 1996), 44.

   a. If so, what was your loss(es)?

   b. If so, how did you cope with the grief?

2. What can you share from your own experience that could help someone else who is experiencing grief?

4

Depression

The Lord is close to the
brokenhearted and saves those
who are crushed in spirit.
—Psalm 34:18 (NIV)

I don't recall ever having suffered from depression.
When a counselor friend of mine where I worked
gave me a pamphlet about depression from Rapha,
a Christ-centered counseling agency, I thought
the pamphlet would be good information for me to
help someone else in the future. Little did I realize
that within a year, I would need the information for
myself.

Sadness is a normal human emotion that we feel from time to time. When that sadness becomes overwhelming, however, and does not go away within a few days or weeks, depression can set in and lead to serious complications if not treated. In this stage, I began to realize the true extent of divorce. William C. Shiel said that depression is "an illness that involves the body, mood, and thoughts[,] and that affects the way a person eats, sleeps, feels about himself or herself, and thinks about things."[27] According to Shiel, the signs and symptoms of depression may include the following:

> (1) Loss of interest in activities that were once interesting or enjoyable … (2) Loss of appetite … (3) Loss of emotional expression … (3) A persistently sad, anxious, or empty mood, (4) Feelings of hopelessness … (5) Social withdrawal, (6) Unusual fatigue … (7) Sleep disturbance and insomnia … (8)

---

[27] William C. Shiel Jr., "Medical Definition of Depression," accessed November 19, 2020), https://www.medicinenet.com/script/main/art.asp?articlekey=2947.

> Trouble concentrating … (8) Unusual restlessness or irritability, and (9) Persistent physical problems.[28]

At one point during the depression stage, I began to experience a rapid heartbeat. As soon as I would go to sleep at night, I would awaken, and my heart would be beating rapidly. Then it was difficult to get back to sleep. When I would eventually get back to sleep again, the process would repeat itself. Seeking professional help, my physician prescribed an antidepressant, which greatly assisted me.

I found that I had to make a conscious effort to focus on Jesus Christ and also to focus on other people rather than being absorbed in myself. To do this, I concentrated on the Word of God and made daily application to my own life.

Paul tells us in Philippians 4:4, "Rejoice in the Lord always. I will say it again: Rejoice!" Also, Paul

---

[28] Shiel, "Medical Definition of Depression."

says in Romans 15:11, "And again, 'Praise the Lord, all you Gentiles; let all the peoples extol him.'"

Then, in 1 Corinthians 10:13, Paul says, "No temptation has overtaken you except what is common to mankind. And God is faithful; he will not let you be tempted beyond what you can bear. But when you are tempted, he will also provide a way out so that you can endure it." Also, the entire book of James tells us to keep our faith in God when we suffer trials and temptations.

Finally, Hebrews 13:15 says, "Keep your lives free from the love of money and be content with what you have, because God has said, 'Never will I leave you; never will I forsake you.'"

Since depression can cause a person to feel powerless, here are a few things to do to take responsibility for your health and regain a feeling of control: (1) exercise; (2) get some sunlight; (3) get enough sleep—but not too much; (4) eat a healthy diet; (5) do things you enjoy; and (6) avoid alcohol and drugs.[29]

The pamphlet from Rapha[30] about depression that my counselor friend gave me listed the following five steps toward relieving the depression:

1. Determine that it is a problem that *must* be dealt with.
2. Accept God's provision of forgiveness for whatever you believe He needs to forgive you for.
3. Ask God who *you* need to forgive—and forgive them based on the fact that God has forgiven them. Christ died for *all* sins including those *against you*!
4. Ask God to show you how you are using anger in your life to protect yourself. Turn

---

[29] "A Depression-Recovery Lifestyle," accessed July 2, 2018, https://www.webmd.com/depression/guide/recovery-lifestyle#1.

[30] *Rapha Reflections*, a Christ-centered counseling agency, n.d. Corporate mailing address: Box 580355, Houston, TX 77258.

from using anger and choose to express God's love as you trust Him for your protection—both physical and emotional.

5. Practice thankfulness.

On a Monday in early March (one year after my husband left), I wrote in my journal some of the things that I was thankful for: (1) God allowing me to grow spiritually; (2) learning to really trust God; (3) developing a special bond with my teenage daughter; (4) greater focus for ministry and missions; (5) providing for me financially; and (6) renewed hope in His promise.

About this same time, a friend shared with me a poem titled "Resent Somebody." A portion of the poem is as follows: "The moment you start to resent a person you become that person's slave. He or she controls your dreams, absorbs your digestion, robs you of your peace of mind and good will, and takes away the pleasure of your work … So, if you want to be a slave, harbor your resentments."[31]

During my pastor's sermon one Sunday morning, I realized that a lot of resentment had built up on my heart during the marital separation. So, I wrote a letter to my estranged husband, asking forgiveness. Forgiveness does not mean that you forget the offense. Instead, forgiveness frees you from any bitterness. In forgiving, you no longer hold the offense against the other person. If you want God to forgive you, you must forgive others. Jesus says in the Lord's Prayer, "And forgive us our debts, as we also have forgiven our debtors" (Matt. 6:12).

On one of my trips to London, England, I had the privilege of attending a seminar by author Jennifer Rees Larcombe. Larcombe not only suffered from a longstanding, crippling illness before God miraculously restored her to good health, but her life

---

[31] "Resent Somebody," author unknown, accessed January 15, 2017, https://answers.yahoo.com/question/index?qid=20071222103612AA9B8pB.

was also shattered by many other disappointments, including a broken marriage. In relation to mending marriages, she made the following statements:

> Sometimes the most difficult "enemy" to forgive is the one to who you were once married. Perhaps it's because love and hate are so closely linked, but some people find it hard to forgive fully after a marriage break-up because they feel that the only possible outcome of forgiveness is getting back together again. When both partners are willing to forgive, this is often the "happy ever after ending," but for many reasons it is not always possible. [32]

She went on to say that "forgiving from the heart is vital—whether such reconciliation means a second honeymoon, or simply the ability to communicate again in a peaceful and friendly manner."[33]

---

[32] Jennifer Rees Larcombe, *Turning Point, Is There Hope for Broken Lives?* (London: Hodder and Stoughton, 1994), 222–223.

[33] Larcombe, *Turning Point*, 223.

Prayer

Thank You, Lord, that You were with me during my times of depression. Thank You for the professional help and friends who surrounded me. Thank You for teaching me how to forgive. Thank You for Your Word that sustained me. Help me to have compassion and empathy for others who suffer from depression. In Jesus's name. Amen!

Reflection Questions

1. Have you ever suffered from depression? If so, did you seek help to overcome the depression?
2. What role did forgiveness play in your recovery from depression?
3. What role does thankfulness play in recovering from depression?
4. Has resentment ever built up in your heart? If so, how did you get rid of the resentment?

5

Rejection

> But he said to me, "My grace is
> sufficient for you, for my power
> is made perfect in weakness.
> Therefore I will boast all the more
> gladly about my weaknesses,
> so that Christ's power may rest
> on me."
> —2 Corinthians 12:9 (NIV)

Rejection was the hardest stage for me. One February afternoon, I was listening to a TV program where the moderator was interviewing women whose husbands had abandoned them. The answer seemed to be to *challenge the pain*.

So, I thought that's what I would do. I tried but really didn't know how.

The next day, I prayed that God would help me to know how to challenge the pain. That afternoon at work, God directed me to a poem by Judith Mammay titled "Forgiveness."[34] As soon as I read the first line, I knew that *forgiveness* was the method of challenging the pain: "Forgiveness is letting go of the pain and accepting what has happened, because it will not change."

I thought I had forgiven him for everything, but evidently, I had not. So, I prayed again—forgiving him for deserting me and for leaving me with the load of all the family responsibilities. From that day forward, I challenged the pain by choosing to forgive him, ceasing to resent him, letting go of the anger for having been injured, and wanting God's best for his life. The last stanza of Mammay's

---

[34] Judith Mammay. "Forgiveness," accessed March 18, 2020, https://works.doklad.ru/view/coRV-Di-t9g.html.

"Forgiveness"[35] poem said: "Forgiveness is starting over with the knowledge that we have gained. I forgive you, and I forgive myself. I hope you can do the same."

To climb out of this stage of rejection, God the Father reminded me of the ultimate rejection by humankind of His only begotten Son. Using a Bible commentary, I began to read scripture after scripture of how Jesus was rejected—and just to think that He gave His life for our redemption, and we still rejected Him.

In the Garden of Gethsemane, the night before His crucifixion, Jesus experienced great agony and pain. He had entered the garden with all the disciples except Judas. (Judas had already begun the betrayal of Jesus.) Jesus knew He would be arrested and crucified soon, and He wanted His

---

[35] Mammay, "Forgiveness."

disciples to remember how dependent He was on His heavenly Father.

Jesus said to the disciples, "Sit here while I go and pray over there. And He took with Him Peter and the two sons of Zebedee, and He began to be sorrowful and deeply distressed" (Matt. 26:36–37). That night Jesus cried out, just like a child, in brokenness and dependency. "O My Father, if it is possible, let this cup pass from Me; nevertheless, not as I will, but as you will" (Matt. 26:39).

On a Friday afternoon in late February, during all my struggles of being a single mom, I read these words of Jesus, and I prayed that same prayer. Instead of God answering the way I thought He would, He gave me the grace to follow the path He would choose for me. When the pain of rejection was so strong, Isaiah 53:3 ministered to me: "He [Jesus] is despised and rejected by men, A Man of sorrows and acquainted with grief … He was despised, and we did not esteem Him."

Matthew (8:34) writes on one occasion: "The whole city came out to meet Jesus. And when they saw him, they begged Him to depart from their region." I noticed that this was just after Jesus had healed two demon-possessed men.

One day, Jesus was talking to the disciples about the coming of the kingdom. Luke (17:25) records Jesus's words: "But first He must suffer many things and be rejected by this generation."

Christ knew He had come to earth to die for every person's sins. So, the *cup* He asked God to remove from Him in Matthew 26 was not death itself. Instead, it was the separation from His Father. His fleshly nature wanted to escape this separation. However, His Godly nature chose to do as the Father willed.

Jesus had a purpose for which He was willing to die. "He suffered betrayal, denial by His friends, humiliation, beatings, spitting, torture, crucifixion, and ultimately death."[36] Philip Yancey said, "When Jesus prayed to the one who could save him from death, he did not get that salvation; he got instead the salvation of the world."[37]

How thankful we need to be that Jesus chose to do the will of the Father! His sufferings and sacrifice were not in vain.

Prayer

Thank You, heavenly Father, that Your grace is sufficient when I feel rejection and that, according to Your Word, Your power is made perfect in my weakness. Help me to remember how much rejection Your only begotten Son experienced when He was here on this earth, and yet He chose to do Your will. In Jesus's name. Amen!

---

[36] Kevin W. McCarthy, *The On-Purpose* Person (Colorado Springs, CO: Pinon Press, 1992), 109.

[37] Philip Yancy, "Jesus' Unanswered Prayers," accessed March 19, 2020, http://www.wordandwork.org/2010/01/jesus-unanswered-prayers/.

Reflection Questions

1. Have you ever felt rejection? If so, what was your reaction?

2. How can forgiveness help you to "challenge the pain" of rejection?

3. What was Jesus's response to rejection?

4. Why is it important that Jesus chose to do the will of the Father?

6

Resistance

Be alert and of sober mind. Your
enemy the devil prowls around like
a roaring lion looking for someone
to devour. Resist him, standing firm
in the faith, because you know that
the family of believers throughout
the world is undergoing the same
kind of sufferings.
—1 Peter 5:8–9 (NIV)

I cannot say that I rebelled, but I can say that I definitely resisted doing ministry alone. My husband and I had made a great team. I accompanied him in three pastorates, and we also traveled with a ministry singing group. I felt that God had put us together to do ministry for His kingdom.

One of the things I learned, though, during this process was that I can make decisions *only* for myself—and not for someone else. I realized that I had to put our broken marriage behind me. Now I needed to focus on taking care of my teenage daughter and also the ministry to which God had called me.

I wrote a chapter titled "The Joy and Ministry Results of the Second Chance" in one of the doctoral textbooks for a university. Sometimes the path you resist can be the second chance of an awesome journey, even though it takes you down a completely different path than what you had in mind. Your epiphany can open doors of opportunity of which you could never dream. God knows to whom you need to minister and influence.

When writing the chapter for the doctoral book, I thought of people in the Bible who took advantage of God's second chance. I also noticed what was accomplished for the kingdom of God as each person obeyed God's leading. One of these biblical characters was Jonah. The remainder of this chapter is an excerpt about Jonah's second chance.[38]

The story of Jonah is a most colorful one. The entire action-packed book, consisting of only forty-eight verses, describes how God gave Jonah a second chance and also how God gave the Ninevites a second chance.

Jonah, chapter 3, begins with God giving Jonah a second chance: "Then the word of the LORD came to Jonah a second time: 'Go to the great city of Nineveh and proclaim to it the message I give you'" (Jonah 3:1–2).

At the beginning of the book, the story began with Jonah's first call: "The word of the Lord

---

[38] Carl Chrisner, ed., *Relationships: The Ministerial Imperative* (Springfield, MO: Global University, 2014), 221–224.

came to Jonah son of Amittai: 'Go to the great city of Nineveh and preach against it, because its wickedness has come up before me'" (Jonah 1:1–2).

Instead of obeying God and taking the warning of judgment to the people of Nineveh, which is in modern-day northern Iraq, Jonah refused and went in the opposite direction. He bought a ticket and boarded a ship bound for Tarshish, which is in modern-day Spain.

What happened? Trouble came, as described in Jonah 1:4–6:

> Then the Lord sent a great wind on the sea, and such a violent storm arose that the ship threatened to break up. All the sailors were afraid and each cried out to his own god. And they threw the cargo into the sea to lighten the ship. But Jonah had gone below deck, where he lay down and fell into a deep sleep. The captain went to him and said, "How can you sleep? Get up and call on

your god! Maybe he will take notice
of us so that we will not perish."

"How convicting is this: that a pagan ship captain had to shake a teacher of God's Word, and wake him up, and beg him to pray for his salvation."[39]

Jonah believed the only solution to the dilemma was to throw him overboard. Jonah said, "Pick me up and throw me into the sea … and it will become calm. I know that it is my fault that this great storm has come upon you" (1:12). Then Jonah (1:15) records, "They took Jonah and threw him overboard, and the raging sea grew calm."

"When it seem[ed] like all hope [was] lost, when it seem[ed] as if Jonah [had] gotten the punishment he deserved[,] we don't see God's wrath, do we?

---

[39] Joel Rosenberg, "Four Reasons Why God Is Shaking America and the World: Text of 'Wake Up Call' Sermon," accessed May 10, 2012, http://flashtrafficblog.wordpress.com/2011/09/13/four-reasons-why-god-is-shaking-america-the-world-text-of-wake-up-call-sermon.

No, we see God's mercy."[40] We see how "the Lord provided a huge fish to swallow Jonah, and Jonah was in the belly of the fish three days and three nights" (Jonah 1:17).

When God first called Jonah to Nineveh, Jonah failed because he refused to go. Notice, however, this failure was not permanent. "It has been said that failure is not fatal and does not have to be final. There is a huge difference between 'failing' at something and being a failure."[41]

Through God's amazing grace, Jonah was given a second chance. "Then the Word of the Lord came to Jonah a second time: 'Go to the great city of Nineveh and proclaim to it the message I give you'" (Jonah 3:1–2). God's plan had not changed. The commission was the same.

---

[40] "A God of Second Chances," accessed August 29, 2012, http://weatherfordfwb.com/mss/Jonah%203%20Sermon.pdf.

[41] "The God of the Second Chance," accessed October 23, 2012, http://storage.cloversites.com/firstbaptistchurchvilonia/documents/04_The%20God%20of%20the%20Second%20Chance.pdf.

The Lord still wanted Jonah to go to Nineveh and warn the people of the coming judgment. This time, Jonah obeyed.

In taking advantage of this second chance that God offered him, Jonah preached one of the shortest evangelical sermons: "Forty more days and Nineveh will be overthrown" (Jonah 3:4). What a miracle resulted! The people of Nineveh heeded God's warning. Jonah (3:5–9) says:

> The Ninevites believed God. A fast was proclaimed, and all of them, from the greatest to the least, put on sackcloth. When Jonah's warning reached the king of Nineveh, he rose from his throne, took off his royal robes, covered himself with sackcloth and sat down in the dust. This is the proclamation he issued in Nineveh: "By the decree of the king and his nobles: Do not let people or animals, herds or flocks, taste anything; do not let them eat or drink. But let people and animals be covered with sackcloth. Let everyone call urgently on God. Let them give up their evil ways and their violence.

> Who knows? God may yet relent and with compassion turn from his fierce anger so that we will not perish."

That's exactly what happened! God saw how the Ninevites repented and turned from their wicked ways. So, He did not destroy them.

The message from the book of Jonah is not only about hearing the Word of God but also obeying it. Even though Jonah ran in the opposite direction at first and great trouble came, he finally listened to the Word of God when God gave him a second chance. As a result, an entire city was saved!

Prayer

Thank You, God, for giving me a second chance at ministry and for being with me every step of the way. Thank You for helping me to focus on the ministry to which You called me. Help me to be patient with others as You work out Your will in their lives. In Jesus's name. Amen!

Reflection Questions

1. Have you ever resisted something that you felt God wanted you to do?

2. Are you resisting God's will now?

3. What can you learn about resisting God's will from the biblical story of Jonah?

7

Acceptance

"For I know the plans I have for you," declares the LORD, plans to prosper you and not to harm you, plans to give you hope and a future.
—Jeremiah 29:11 (NIV)

The first part of the acceptance stage was the acknowledgment that my husband was not returning. God directed me to a colleague's office one autumn day in November. As we talked about the influence of choices in our lives, he shared with me Portia Nelson's "There's a Hole in My Sidewalk, Autobiography in Five Short Chapters." Chapter 1 said, "I walk down the street. There is a deep hole in the sidewalk. I fall in. I am lost … I am helpless. It isn't my fault. It takes forever to find a way out."[42]

Nelson said in chapter 2 that you walk down the street with the deep hole in the sidewalk, and you pretend not to see it. So, you fall in again. The last part of the stanza revealed, "I can't believe I am in this same place. But it isn't my fault. It still takes a long time to get out."[43]

Chapter 3 reflected that you walk down the street with the deep hole in the sidewalk. You see the hole, but you still fall in because it is a habit. At least, though, your eyes are open, and you know where you are. Since you recognize that it is your own fault, you get out immediately.[44]

Nelson shortened chapters 3 and 4. In chapter 4, you walk down the street with the deep hole

[42] Portia Nelson, "There's a Hole in My Sidewalk, Autobiography in Five Short Chapters," accessed March 19, 2020, https://palousemindfulness.com/docs/autobio_5chapters.pdf.

[43] Nelson, "Hole in My Sidewalk."

[44] Nelson, "Hole in My Sidewalk."

in the sidewalk, but you walk around it. The poet concluded chapter 5 with "I walk down another street." [45]

Metaphors help us understand life. They compare "dissimilar things on the basis of some underlying commonality, [and] a new insight or broadened understanding is created."[46]

In this poem, Nelson compared life to a stroll down a sidewalk that is somewhat hazardous. Chapter 1 allowed you to reflect on your own journey:

> What has your experience been? What good times have you had? Do you remember some of the difficult times? Most importantly consider the question, "Have you ever fallen in to one of the holes in the sidewalk?" Have you been minding your own business when the bottom fell out? Have you suddenly found yourself in a pit of frustration, anger, anxiety,

---

[45] Nelson, "Hole in My Sidewalk."

[46] "The Sidewalk of Life," accessed March 19, 2020, http://www.lessons4living.com/sidewalk_of_life.htm#Reference#Reference.

resentment, grief, or despair? Have you confronted loss, change, and challenge that caught you by surprise and seemed out of your control?[47]

Once you fall into the hole, you must struggle to get out. This struggle, though, allows you to grow and mature.

Consider in chapter 2 whether you have ever "found yourself in exactly the same hole more than once"[48] and wonder why this happened to you.

1. Are you in exactly the same bad relationship (but with a different person) for the twentieth time? Are you starting to wonder how all of these jerks *find* you?

2. How is it that you always get into the same type of conflict with the boss? She is so negative and critical and always expects so much. She makes you feel miserable.

---

[47] Nelson, "Hole in My Sidewalk."

[48] Nelson, "Hole in My Sidewalk."

3. Maybe you are in the midst of the exact "word for word" argument with your spouse for the ten thousandth time. He says *this* and you say *that* just like you always do and you fall into the hole once again.

4. Your son, mother, sister, or brother does that thing that they always do. It pushes your buttons and you respond as you always do. The cycle of conflict begins once again.[49]

You wish others would just "act right," and often you work hard to get them to change.

Chapter 3 is a wake-up call. If you recognize that there is a pattern in your life, take responsibility for yourself. McCarthy said, "Once you accept responsibility for yourself, other people are powerless to impose their agendas and expectations

---

[49] Nelson, "Hole in My Sidewalk."

on you. That is freedom and power. Freedom to choose, consistent with your purpose."[50]

Chapter 4 is a new chapter. You avoid the holes—at least on that street. You respond to life differently. "An on-purpose person accepts personal responsibility for discovering his or her unique purpose."[51]

Chapter 5 begins with a new day because you change streets. Will there be holes on this street? Sure. Will you fall in? Make wise choices. Take responsibility for your choices. Then you will grow.

The second part of the acceptance stage for me was accepting the call of God on my life and me ministering without my husband. On a cold February day, God called me to preach. It was in a chapel service at the university where I taught. Little did I realize that my husband, who had been

---

[50] Kevin W. McCarthy, *The On-Purpose Person, Making Your Life Make Sense* (Colorado Springs, CO: Pinon Press, 1992), 114.

[51] McCarthy, *On-Purpose Person*, 114.

a minister for more than twenty years, was already making plans to leave our marriage. On that day in February, I felt the call to pulpit ministry and also felt that missions would be a part of my ministry. Since that time, God has opened doors for ministry in China, the Caribbean, Cuba, Egypt, El Salvador, England, Ghana, the Holy Land, India, Jamaica, Kenya, Malaysia, the Mediterranean, South Africa, and Tanzania as well as in the United States. I have even served as a Protestant chaplain on a cruise ship.

At the time that I was completing the application for my ministerial credentials, one of my younger brothers, who is also a minister, told me he felt that part of my ministry would be to women, which proved to be a prophetic word. God has given me the privilege not only to minister one-on-one with women but also to speak at many women's conferences. To God be the glory!

Prayer

Thank You, Lord, for helping me to accept Your call to ministry. Ministering to others in Your kingdom around the world has been a privilege. Help me to always listen to Your voice as You guide me through life and accept the plans that You have for my life. In Jesus's name. Amen!

Reflection Questions

1. As you reflect on your life's journey, have you accepted responsibility for yourself?

2. How have you grown by accepting responsibility for yourself and your actions?

3. Are you willing to accept the plans that God has for your life?

8

Letting Go

And we know that in all things God
works for the good of those who
love him, who have been called
according to his purpose.
—Romans 8:28 (NIV)

I prayed as I went through this dark three-year tunnel of separation that I would learn what God wanted to teach me and that I would come forth as pure gold, just as Job 23:10 says, "But He knows the way that I take; When He has tested me, I shall come forth as gold."

I believe one of the reasons God allowed me to walk through this three-year storm was to know the horrible pain that thousands of others experience. When someone you love walks out on you, there is a pain that is indescribable. But we have to remember that Jesus experienced much rejection from those He loved and for whom He gave His life.

I also believe that God wanted me to experience the victories that are possible through "Christ who gives me strength" (Phil. 4:13) and "God's peace, which exceeds anything we can understand" (Phil. 4:7). God went before me every step of my path. Because God answered so many prayers for me and brought victory in seemingly impossible situations, I know that He will do the same for you.

During the final phase of this part of my life, a friend shared with me the poem "Letting Go." The first part of the poem said, "To 'let go' does not mean to stop caring, it means I can't do it for someone else. To 'let go' is not to cut myself off, it's the realization I can't control another. To 'let go' is not to enable, but to allow learning from natural consequences. To 'let go' is to admit powerlessness, which means the outcome is not in my hands."[52]

The poet went on to say, "To 'let go' is not to try to change or blame another, it's to make the most of myself … is not to care for, but to care about … is not to fix, but to be supportive."[53]

The concluding lines gave the following admonition, "To 'let go' is not to regret the past, but to grow and live for the future. To 'let go' is to fear less, and love more."[54]

In letting go, I learned to pray about every situation. In the absence of my natural husband, I found that God was my husband and provided for me. Isaiah 54:5 says, "For your Maker is your husband—the Lord Almighty is his name." This passage was written to Israel, but I believe that the

---

[52] "Letting Go," accessed November 25, 2020, https://www.theribbon.com/poetry/lettinggo.php.

[53] "Letting Go," accessed November 25, 2020.

[54] "Letting Go," accessed November 25, 2020.

metaphor being used here can also apply to those who are divorced or widowed today.

Jesus Christ, the Son of God, has been with me every step of the way. My older brother told me that before I ever reached a difficult point in my life, Jesus was already there because He knew I would pass that way. How often I am reminded of Jesus's promise in Hebrews 13:5, "Never will I leave you; never will I forsake you."

When Jesus ascended to the Father, He promised to send us a comforter. John (14:26) tells us, "But the Counselor [Comforter], the Holy Spirit, whom the Father will send in my name, will teach you all things and will remind you of everything I have said to you." That counselor gave me wisdom and guidance through every situation.

What a privilege it has been to consider it pure joy when I faced trials of many kinds (James 1:2).

Prayer

Thank You, Jesus, for being with me every step of the way and for the promise in Your Word to never leave me or forsake me. Thank You, Holy Spirit, for Your comfort and counsel and for helping me to let go. Help me to always pray about every situation and listen to Your wisdom. In Jesus's name. Amen!

Reflection Questions

1. Which part of the "Letting Go" poem applies to you?
2. How can prayer help you to let go?

Chapter Scriptures (NIV)

Chapter 1   Denial

Psalm 16:7–8
I will praise the LORD, who counsels me; even at night my heart instructs me.
I keep my eyes always on the LORD. With him at my right hand, I will not be shaken.

Matthew 16:24
Then Jesus said to his disciples, "Whoever wants to be my disciple must deny themselves and take up their cross and follow me."

Luke 12:8-9
"I tell you, whoever publicly acknowledges me before others, the Son of Man will also acknowledge before the angels of God. But whoever disowns me before others will be disowned before the angels of God."

2 Timothy 2:12
If we endure, we will also reign with him. If we disown him, he will also disown us.

Chapter 2   Reconciliation

Ephesians 4:32
Be kind and compassionate to one another, forgiving each other, just as in Christ God forgave you.

Colossians 3:13
Bear with each other and forgive one another if any of you has a grievance against someone. Forgive as the Lord forgave you.

Hebrews 12:14
Make every effort to live in peace with everyone and to be holy; without holiness no one will see the Lord.

Chapter 3   Grief

Isaiah 41:10
So do not fear, for I am with you; do not be dismayed, for I am your God. I will strengthen you and help you; I will uphold you with my righteous right hand.

Isaiah 43:2
When you pass through the waters, I will be with you; and when you pass through the rivers, they will not sweep over you. When you walk through the fire, you will not be burned; the flames will not set you ablaze.

Isaiah 49:13
Shout for joy, you heavens; rejoice, you earth; burst into song, you mountains!

For the LORD comforts his people and will have compassion on his afflicted ones.

2 Corinthians 1:3-4
Praise be to the God and Father of our Lord Jesus Christ, the Father of compassion and the God of all comfort, who comforts us in all our troubles, so that we can comfort those in any trouble with the comfort we ourselves receive from God.

Chapter 4   Depression

Psalm 34:18
The LORD is close to the brokenhearted and saves those who are crushed in spirit.

Psalm 40:1–3
I waited patiently for the LORD; he turned to me and heard my cry.
He lifted me out of the slimy pit, out of the mud and mire; he set my feet on a rock and gave me a firm place to stand.
He put a new song in my mouth, a hymn of praise to our God. Many will see and fear the LORD and put their trust in him.

Psalm 143:7
Answer me quickly, LORD; my spirit fails. Do not hide your face from me or I will be like those who go down to the pit.

Proverbs 12:25

Anxiety weighs down the heart, but a kind word cheers it up.

1 Peter 5:6–7

Humble yourselves, therefore, under God's mighty hand, that he may lift you up in due time. Cast all your anxiety on him because he cares for you.

Chapter 5   Rejection

Isaiah 53:3

He was despised and rejected by mankind, a man of suffering, and familiar with pain. Like one from whom people hide their faces he was despised, and we held him in low esteem.

Romans 15:13

May the God of hope fill you with all joy and peace as you trust in him, so that you may overflow with hope by the power of the Holy Spirit.

1 Peter 5: 8

Be alert and of sober mind. Your enemy the devil prowls around like a roaring lion looking for someone to devour.

2 Corinthians 12:9

But he said to me, "My grace is sufficient for you, for my power is made perfect in weakness." Therefore I will boast all the more gladly about my weaknesses, so that Christ's power may rest on me.

Chapter 6   Resistance

Isaiah 53:7–9

He was oppressed and afflicted, yet he did not open his mouth; he was led like a lamb to the slaughter, and as a sheep before its shearers is silent, so he did not open his mouth.

By oppression and judgment he was taken away. Yet who of his generation protested? For he was cut off from the land of the living; for the transgression of my people he was punished.

He was assigned a grave with the wicked, and with the rich in his death, though he had done no violence, nor was any deceit in his mouth.

1 Corinthians 10:13

No temptation has overtaken you except what is common to mankind. And God is faithful; he will not let you be tempted beyond what you can bear. But when you are tempted, he will also provide a way out so that you can endure it.

Ephesians 6:11–13

Put on the full armor of God, so that you can take your stand against the devil's schemes. For our struggle is not against flesh and blood, but against the rulers, against the authorities, against the powers of this dark world and against the spiritual forces of evil in the heavenly realms. Therefore put on the full armor of God, so that when the day of evil comes, you may be able to stand your ground, and after you have done everything, to stand.

James 4:6

But he gives us more grace. That is why Scripture says: "God opposes the proud but shows favor to the humble."

1 Peter 5:8–9

Be alert and of sober mind. Your enemy the devil prowls around like a roaring lion looking for someone to devour. Resist him, standing firm in the faith, because you know that the family of believers throughout the world is undergoing the same kind of sufferings.

Chapter 7   Acceptance

Jeremiah 29:11

For I know the plans I have for you," declares the LORD, "plans to prosper you and not to harm you, plans to give you hope and a future.

Luke 9:23–24

Then he said to them all: "Whoever wants to be my disciple must deny themselves and take up their cross daily and follow me.

For whoever wants to save their life will lose it, but whoever loses their life for me will save it.

1 Thessalonians 5:18

Give thanks in all circumstances; for this is God's will for you in Christ Jesus.

Chapter 8   Letting Go

Proverbs 3:5–6
Trust in the LORD with all your heart and lean not on your own understanding; in all your ways submit to him, and he will make your paths straight.

Romans 8:28
And we know that in all things God works for the good of those who love him, who have been called according to his purpose.

James 1:5
If any of you lacks wisdom, you should ask God, who gives generously to all without finding fault, and it will be given to you.

Bibliography

American Greetings card.

Author's email to friend.

Chrisner, Carl, ed. *Relationships: The Ministerial Imperative.* Springfield, Missouri: Global University, 2014.

Classic Elegance. "A Loving Message for My Wife on Her Birthday, These I Can Promise*."* Cleveland, Ohio: American Greetings.

Crouch, Andraé. "The Broken Vessel." Pacific City, Oregon: Manna Music, Inc., 1968.

"A Depression-Recovery Lifestyle." Accessed July 2, 2018. https://www.webmd.com/depression/guide/recovery-lifestyle#1.

Friend's email to author.

"A God of Second Chances." Accessed August 29, 2012. http://weatherfordfwb.com/mss/Jonah%203%20Sermon.pdf.

"The God of the Second Chance." Accessed October 23, 2012. http://storage.cloversites.com/firstbaptistchurchvilonia/documents/04_The%20God%20of%20the%20Second%20Chance.pdf.

Gottman, John. The Marriage Clinic: A Scientifically Based Marital Therapy. New York: Norton, 1999. Quoted in "Healing Love's Wounds." Accessed November 12, 2020. https://emerge.org/healing-loves-wounds-a-pastoral-approach-to-marriage-divorce-and-remarriage-counseling/.

"Healing Love's Wounds." Accessed November 12, 2020. https://emerge.org/healing-loves-wounds-a-pastoral-approach-to-marriage-divorce-and-remarriage-counseling/.

"I Came to Glorify His Name." Accessed January 4, 2019. http://stevencarr.com/songs/worshipsongs.

Janney, Ronnie M. "Take Things One Day at a Time." One Step at a Time. Boulder, Colorado: Blue Mountain Press, 1994.

Larcombe, Jennifer Rees. Turning Point, Is There Hope for Broken Lives? London: Hodder and Stoughton, 1994.

"Letting Go." Accessed November 25, 2020. https://www.theribbon.com/poetry/lettinggo.php.

McCarthy, Kevin W. *The On-Purpose Person, Making Your Life Make Sense*. Colorado Springs, Colorado: Pinon Press, 1992.

Mammay, Judith. "Forgiveness." Accessed March 18, 2020. https://works.doklad.ru/view/coRV-Di-t9g.html.

Moses, Ken. "The Impact of Childhood Disability: The Parent's Struggle." Accessed November 19, 2020. http://www.pent.ca.gov/beh/dis/parentstruggle_DK.pdf.

Nelson, Portia. "There's a Hole in My Sidewalk, Autobiography in Five Short Chapters." Accessed March 19, 2020. https://palousemindfulness.com/docs/autobio 5chapters.pdf.

Rapha Reflections. A Christ-centered counseling agency. Corporate mailing address: Box 580355, Houston, TX 77258.

"Resent Somebody." Author unknown. Accessed January 15, 2017. https://answers.yahoo.com/question/index?qid=20071222103612AA9B8pB.

Robinson, Haddon W. *Grief*. Grand Rapids, Michigan: Discovery House Publishers, 1996.

Rosenberg, Joel. "Four Reasons Why God Is Shaking America and the World: Text of 'Wake-Up Call' Sermon." Accessed May 10, 2012. http://flashtrafficblog.wordpress.com/2011/09/13/four-reasons-why-god-is-shaking-america-the-world-text-of-wake-up-call-sermon.

Shiel Jr., William C. "Medical Definition of Depression." Accessed November 19, 2020, https://www.medicinenet.com/script/main/art.asp?articlekey=2947.

"The Sidewalk of Life." Accessed March 19, 2020. http://www.lessons4living.com/sidewalk_of_life.htm#Reference#Reference.

Smoke, Jim. *Growing through Divorce.* Eugene, Oklahoma: Harvest House Publishers, 1995.

Wolfelt, Alan D. "Helping a Friend in Grief." Accessed November 19, 2020. https://www.monarchsociety.com/griefarticle/article/helping10.

Wood, George O. *A Psalm in Your Heart, Volume 1 Psalms 1-75.* Springfield, Missouri: Gospel Publishing House, 1997.

Wymer, Laurie. "My Authentic Self." *One Step at a Time*. Boulder, Colorado: Blue Mountain Press, 1994.

Yancey, Philip. "Jesus' Unanswered Prayers." Accessed March 19, 2020. http://www.wordandwork. org/2010/01/jesus-unanswered-prayers/.

About the Author

Mary Slankster, Ed.D., has served as an ordained minister, conference speaker, and short-term missionary, and she also ministers regularly in churches. She earned her Ed.D. at Texas A&M University–Commerce and has taught in both public schools and universities. She and her husband, Dwayne, reside in northeastern Texas.